50 Japanese Premium Dinner Restaurant Dishes

By: Kelly Johnson

Table of Contents

- Wagyu Beef Steak
- Omakase Sushi
- Sashimi Platter
- Kaiseki
- Unagi Don (Grilled Eel Rice Bowl)
- Tempura (Assorted)
- A5 Wagyu Beef Shabu-Shabu
- Miso Soup with Clams
- Kaisen Don (Seafood Rice Bowl)
- Chirashi Sushi
- Sukiyaki
- Beef Tataki
- Ebi Tempura
- Tonkatsu (Pork Cutlet)
- Black Cod Miso
- Ramen with Chashu Pork
- Yakitori (Grilled Chicken Skewers)
- Gindara Saikyo Yaki (Miso-Marinated Black Cod)
- Shabu-Shabu with Vegetables
- Soba Noodles with Tempura
- Gyudon (Beef Bowl)
- Chirashi Don with Tuna and Salmon
- Tofu Chawanmushi
- Gyoza (Dumplings)
- Tonkotsu Ramen
- Seared Scallops with Soy Sauce
- Crab Croquette
- Tori Katsu (Chicken Cutlet)
- Ikura Don (Salmon Roe Rice Bowl)
- Uni Sushi (Sea Urchin)
- Tamago (Japanese Omelette)
- Ebi Nigiri (Shrimp Sushi)
- Miso-Marinated Eggplant
- Ikura Chawanmushi
- Lobster Tempura
- Yuba (Tofu Skin) with Ponzu Sauce

- Oysters with Ponzu Sauce
- Agedashi Tofu
- Hokkaido King Crab Legs
- Sea Bass in Yuzu Soy Sauce
- Japanese Beef Katsu
- Sushi Rolls with Truffle Oil
- Kurage (Jellyfish) Salad
- Dashi Soup with Tofu
- Shoyu Ramen with Soft-Boiled Egg
- Kani Salad (Crab Salad)
- Shrimp and Vegetable Tempura Udon
- Tataki-style Tuna
- Chilled Soba with Tsuyu Sauce
- Gyu Kushi (Grilled Beef Skewers)

Wagyu Beef Steak

Ingredients:

- 2 A5 Wagyu beef steaks
- Salt and pepper, to taste
- 2 tbsp olive oil or vegetable oil
- 2 tbsp unsalted butter
- 2 cloves garlic, smashed
- Fresh thyme or rosemary (optional)

Instructions:

1. Remove the Wagyu steaks from the fridge and let them rest at room temperature for 20 minutes.
2. Season the steaks with salt and pepper on both sides.
3. Heat the oil in a heavy skillet or cast-iron pan over medium-high heat.
4. Once the oil is hot, add the steaks and sear for 2-3 minutes on each side, or until browned and crispy.
5. Add butter, garlic, and thyme/rosemary to the pan. Baste the steaks with the melted butter for another 1-2 minutes.
6. Remove from the pan and let the steaks rest for 5 minutes before serving.

Omakase Sushi

Ingredients:

- Sushi-grade fish (e.g., tuna, salmon, yellowtail, etc.)
- Sushi rice (prepared with rice vinegar, sugar, and salt)
- Nori (seaweed)
- Wasabi and soy sauce (for serving)
- Pickled ginger (for serving)

Instructions:

1. Prepare sushi rice according to the package instructions and season it with rice vinegar, sugar, and salt.
2. Slice the fish into thin, bite-sized pieces.
3. Form small, oval-shaped portions of sushi rice.
4. Place a slice of fish over each rice portion, gently pressing down.
5. Serve the sushi with wasabi, soy sauce, and pickled ginger on the side.

Sashimi Platter

Ingredients:

- Sushi-grade fish (e.g., tuna, salmon, yellowtail, etc.)
- Wasabi and soy sauce (for serving)
- Pickled ginger (for serving)

Instructions:

1. Slice the sushi-grade fish into thin, even slices.
2. Arrange the fish on a platter, creating an appealing layout.
3. Serve with wasabi, soy sauce, and pickled ginger on the side.

Kaiseki

Ingredients:

- Assorted seasonal ingredients (e.g., fish, vegetables, tofu, rice, etc.)
- Miso soup, pickles, rice, and a main protein (e.g., grilled fish or beef)
- Dishes such as sashimi, simmered vegetables, and tempura

Instructions:

1. Kaiseki is a multi-course meal, so prepare each dish individually, focusing on seasonal ingredients.
2. Start with an appetizer like sashimi or pickles, followed by a soup like miso soup.
3. Serve a main dish such as grilled fish, Wagyu beef, or tempura.
4. End the meal with a dessert, such as a sweet tofu or seasonal fruit.

Unagi Don (Grilled Eel Rice Bowl)

Ingredients:

- 2 fillets of unagi (grilled eel)
- 2 cups cooked sushi rice
- 1/4 cup unagi sauce (made with soy sauce, sugar, mirin, and sake)
- Toasted sesame seeds (optional)
- Pickled ginger (for garnish)

Instructions:

1. Grill the unagi fillets until heated through and slightly caramelized.
2. Prepare sushi rice and place it in a bowl.
3. Drizzle unagi sauce over the rice and place the grilled eel on top.
4. Garnish with sesame seeds and pickled ginger.

Tempura (Assorted)

Ingredients:

- 1 cup all-purpose flour
- 1 egg
- 1/2 cup cold water
- 1/4 tsp baking soda
- Assorted vegetables (e.g., sweet potatoes, zucchini, eggplant, mushrooms)
- Shrimp (peeled and deveined)
- Vegetable oil for frying
- Tempura dipping sauce (soy sauce, mirin, and dashi)

Instructions:

1. Heat the oil in a large pot for frying.
2. Mix the flour, egg, water, and baking soda together to create the tempura batter. It should be lumpy and cold.
3. Dip the vegetables and shrimp into the batter and fry in the hot oil until golden and crispy.
4. Drain on paper towels and serve with tempura dipping sauce.

A5 Wagyu Beef Shabu-Shabu

Ingredients:

- 1 lb A5 Wagyu beef (sliced thinly)
- 4 cups dashi broth
- Assorted vegetables (e.g., bok choy, mushrooms, tofu, napa cabbage)
- Soy sauce, mirin, and sesame sauce for dipping

Instructions:

1. Prepare the dashi broth by heating water with dashi powder.
2. Arrange the sliced Wagyu beef and vegetables on platters.
3. Bring the dashi broth to a boil in a fondue pot or large pot.
4. Dip the Wagyu beef and vegetables into the boiling broth for a few seconds until cooked to your liking.
5. Serve with soy sauce, mirin, and sesame sauce for dipping.

Miso Soup with Clams

Ingredients:

- 4 cups dashi broth
- 2 tbsp miso paste
- 1/2 lb fresh clams
- 1/4 cup tofu (cubed)
- 2 green onions, sliced

Instructions:

1. Bring the dashi broth to a boil in a pot.
2. Add miso paste and stir until dissolved.
3. Add the clams and cook until they open.
4. Add tofu cubes and green onions and cook for another 2-3 minutes.
5. Serve hot.

Kaisen Don (Seafood Rice Bowl)

Ingredients:

- 2 cups cooked sushi rice
- Assorted sashimi-grade seafood (e.g., tuna, salmon, yellowtail, shrimp, scallops)
- 1 tbsp soy sauce
- 1 tsp wasabi
- Pickled ginger (for garnish)
- Fresh cilantro or seaweed (optional)

Instructions:

1. Place the sushi rice in a bowl and top with slices of fresh seafood.
2. Drizzle soy sauce over the seafood and add a small amount of wasabi.
3. Garnish with pickled ginger and fresh cilantro or seaweed if desired.

Chirashi Sushi

Ingredients:

- 2 cups cooked sushi rice
- Assorted sashimi-grade fish (e.g., tuna, salmon, yellowtail, shrimp, and roe)
- 1/4 cup julienned vegetables (e.g., cucumber, carrots, radish)
- Soy sauce, to taste
- Pickled ginger (for garnish)

Instructions:

1. Prepare the sushi rice and place it in a bowl.
2. Arrange slices of sashimi-grade fish and julienned vegetables on top of the rice.
3. Drizzle with soy sauce and serve with pickled ginger on the side.

Sukiyaki

Ingredients:

- 1 lb thinly sliced beef (ribeye or sirloin)
- 1 onion, sliced
- 1 cup shiitake mushrooms, sliced
- 1/2 cup tofu, cubed
- 2 cups napa cabbage, chopped
- 2 tbsp soy sauce
- 2 tbsp mirin
- 1 tbsp sake
- 1 tbsp sugar
- 4 cups dashi broth
- 2 green onions, sliced
- 1 egg (for dipping, optional)
- 2 tbsp vegetable oil

Instructions:

1. Heat oil in a large skillet or hot pot over medium-high heat.
2. Add the beef and brown it on both sides, then remove and set aside.
3. Add the onion, mushrooms, tofu, cabbage, and green onions to the pot.
4. In a bowl, combine soy sauce, mirin, sake, sugar, and dashi broth. Pour the mixture into the pot and bring to a simmer.
5. Add the beef back to the pot and simmer for another 10-15 minutes until the beef is tender and the flavors meld.
6. Serve hot, with a raw egg for dipping (optional).

Beef Tataki

Ingredients:

- 8 oz beef tenderloin (or sirloin)
- 2 tbsp soy sauce
- 1 tbsp rice vinegar
- 1 tbsp mirin
- 1 tsp sesame oil
- 1/4 cup green onions, sliced
- 1 tsp grated ginger
- 1 tbsp sesame seeds
- 1 tbsp vegetable oil (for searing)

Instructions:

1. Heat a pan with vegetable oil over high heat.
2. Season the beef with salt and pepper, then sear on all sides for about 2-3 minutes per side until browned.
3. Remove the beef and let it cool to room temperature, then refrigerate for 20 minutes to firm it up.
4. Slice the beef thinly and arrange it on a plate.
5. Mix soy sauce, rice vinegar, mirin, sesame oil, ginger, and green onions in a small bowl. Drizzle the sauce over the beef.
6. Sprinkle with sesame seeds and serve immediately.

Ebi Tempura

Ingredients:

- 8-10 large shrimp (peeled and deveined, with tails on)
- 1 cup all-purpose flour
- 1/2 cup cornstarch
- 1 egg
- 1 cup ice-cold sparkling water
- 1/2 tsp baking powder
- Vegetable oil for frying
- Tempura dipping sauce (soy sauce, mirin, and dashi)

Instructions:

1. Heat oil in a large pot for frying.
2. In a bowl, whisk together flour, cornstarch, egg, and baking powder. Gradually add sparkling water to make a light batter.
3. Dip each shrimp in the batter and fry in the hot oil until golden and crispy, about 2-3 minutes.
4. Drain on paper towels and serve with tempura dipping sauce.

Tonkatsu (Pork Cutlet)

Ingredients:

- 4 pork cutlets (boneless, about 1/2-inch thick)
- Salt and pepper, to taste
- 1/2 cup all-purpose flour
- 2 eggs, beaten
- 1 cup panko breadcrumbs
- Vegetable oil for frying
- Tonkatsu sauce (for serving)

Instructions:

1. Season the pork cutlets with salt and pepper.
2. Dredge the pork in flour, dip in the beaten eggs, then coat with panko breadcrumbs.
3. Heat oil in a deep pan over medium heat. Fry the pork cutlets until golden brown and crispy, about 4-5 minutes per side.
4. Drain on paper towels and slice. Serve with tonkatsu sauce.

Black Cod Miso

Ingredients:

- 2 black cod fillets
- 1/4 cup white miso paste
- 2 tbsp sake
- 2 tbsp mirin
- 1 tbsp sugar
- 1 tbsp soy sauce
- 1 tsp sesame oil

Instructions:

1. Mix the miso paste, sake, mirin, sugar, soy sauce, and sesame oil in a bowl.
2. Marinate the black cod fillets in the miso mixture for 2-4 hours.
3. Preheat the oven to 400°F (200°C).
4. Place the marinated fish on a baking sheet and broil for about 8-10 minutes until the fish is cooked and caramelized on top.
5. Serve hot with rice.

Ramen with Chashu Pork

Ingredients:

- 4 cups chicken or pork broth
- 2 servings of ramen noodles
- 1/2 lb pork belly (for chashu)
- 2 tbsp soy sauce
- 2 tbsp mirin
- 1 tbsp sake
- 1 tsp sugar
- 2 green onions, sliced
- 2 soft-boiled eggs
- Nori (seaweed), for garnish

Instructions:

1. To make the chashu pork: braise the pork belly in soy sauce, mirin, sake, and sugar for about 2 hours on low heat, until tender. Let it cool and slice thinly.
2. Cook ramen noodles according to package instructions.
3. In a separate pot, heat the broth and season with soy sauce and mirin.
4. Divide the noodles into bowls, pour hot broth over them, and top with chashu pork, sliced green onions, soft-boiled eggs, and nori.

Yakitori (Grilled Chicken Skewers)

Ingredients:

- 1 lb chicken thighs (boneless, skinless), cut into bite-sized pieces
- 1/4 cup soy sauce
- 2 tbsp mirin
- 1 tbsp sake
- 1 tbsp sugar
- 2 tbsp vegetable oil
- 8-10 skewers (soaked in water for 30 minutes)
- Salt and pepper, to taste

Instructions:

1. Combine soy sauce, mirin, sake, and sugar in a small saucepan. Bring to a simmer and cook for 5-10 minutes until thickened.
2. Thread the chicken onto the skewers.
3. Brush the chicken with the marinade and grill over medium-high heat, turning occasionally until cooked through (about 10 minutes).
4. Serve with a sprinkle of salt and pepper.

Gindara Saikyo Yaki (Miso-Marinated Black Cod)

Ingredients:

- 2 black cod fillets
- 1/4 cup white miso paste
- 2 tbsp sake
- 2 tbsp mirin
- 2 tbsp sugar
- 1 tbsp soy sauce

Instructions:

1. Mix the miso paste, sake, mirin, sugar, and soy sauce in a bowl to make the marinade.
2. Marinate the black cod fillets for 2-4 hours in the refrigerator.
3. Preheat the oven to 400°F (200°C).
4. Broil the marinated fish for 10 minutes, or until the fish is caramelized and cooked through.
5. Serve hot with steamed rice.

Shabu-Shabu with Vegetables

Ingredients:

- 1 lb thinly sliced beef (shabu-shabu grade)
- 4 cups dashi broth
- 1/2 lb napa cabbage, chopped
- 1/2 lb shiitake mushrooms, sliced
- 1/2 lb tofu, cubed
- 1/2 cup green onions, sliced
- Soy sauce, for dipping
- Sesame sauce, for dipping

Instructions:

1. Prepare the dashi broth and bring it to a simmer in a hot pot.
2. Arrange the sliced beef and vegetables on platters.
3. Bring the broth to a boil and dip the beef and vegetables into the pot for a few seconds until cooked to your liking.
4. Serve with soy sauce and sesame sauce for dipping.

Soba Noodles with Tempura

Ingredients:

- 2 servings soba noodles
- 8-10 shrimp (peeled and deveined)
- 1/2 cup all-purpose flour (for tempura)
- 1/2 cup cornstarch (for tempura)
- 1 egg (for tempura batter)
- 1 cup cold sparkling water (for tempura batter)
- Vegetable oil for frying
- Soy sauce (for dipping)
- Tempura dipping sauce (soy sauce, mirin, dashi, and sugar)

Instructions:

1. Cook the soba noodles according to package instructions. Drain and set aside.
2. In a bowl, mix flour and cornstarch. Add the egg and cold sparkling water to create a light batter.
3. Heat oil in a deep pan over medium-high heat.
4. Dip shrimp into the batter and fry until golden and crispy (2-3 minutes).
5. Serve soba noodles topped with tempura shrimp and tempura dipping sauce on the side.

Gyudon (Beef Bowl)

Ingredients:

- 1 lb thinly sliced beef (such as ribeye)
- 1 onion, thinly sliced
- 1/4 cup soy sauce
- 1/4 cup mirin
- 2 tbsp sugar
- 1 cup dashi broth
- 2 tsp sake
- 2 cups cooked rice (for serving)
- Green onions, sliced (for garnish)

Instructions:

1. In a large pan, sauté the onions until softened.
2. Add the beef and cook until browned.
3. In a bowl, combine soy sauce, mirin, sugar, dashi, and sake. Pour the mixture over the beef and onions.
4. Simmer for 10 minutes, allowing the flavors to meld.
5. Serve the beef mixture over a bowl of hot rice, garnished with sliced green onions.

Chirashi Don with Tuna and Salmon

Ingredients:

- 2 cups sushi rice, cooked and seasoned
- 4 oz sushi-grade tuna, sliced
- 4 oz sushi-grade salmon, sliced
- 1/4 cup cucumber, julienned
- 1/4 cup avocado, diced
- 1 tbsp sesame seeds
- 1 tbsp soy sauce
- 1 tbsp rice vinegar
- 1 tsp wasabi (optional)

Instructions:

1. In a bowl, place a bed of sushi rice.
2. Arrange the sliced tuna, salmon, cucumber, and avocado on top.
3. Sprinkle with sesame seeds and drizzle with soy sauce and rice vinegar.
4. Serve with a small amount of wasabi if desired.

Tofu Chawanmushi

Ingredients:

- 1/2 cup soft tofu, mashed
- 2 eggs
- 2 cups dashi broth
- 1 tbsp soy sauce
- 1 tbsp mirin
- 1/4 cup shiitake mushrooms, sliced
- 2 tbsp cooked shrimp (optional)
- 1/4 cup green onions, chopped
- Salt, to taste

Instructions:

1. In a bowl, whisk together eggs, dashi, soy sauce, mirin, and salt.
2. Add the mashed tofu and mix well.
3. Strain the mixture to remove any large particles.
4. Pour into small cups and add a few slices of shiitake mushrooms and shrimp.
5. Steam the cups in a steamer for about 15-20 minutes until set.
6. Garnish with green onions and serve.

Gyoza (Dumplings)

Ingredients:

- 1/2 lb ground pork
- 1/2 cup cabbage, finely chopped
- 2 cloves garlic, minced
- 1 tbsp ginger, grated
- 2 tbsp soy sauce
- 1 tbsp sesame oil
- 1/4 cup green onions, chopped
- 20 gyoza wrappers
- Vegetable oil for frying
- Soy sauce for dipping

Instructions:

1. In a bowl, combine ground pork, cabbage, garlic, ginger, soy sauce, sesame oil, and green onions.
2. Place a spoonful of the mixture in the center of each gyoza wrapper. Wet the edges with water and fold the wrapper to seal.
3. Heat a little oil in a pan and fry the gyoza until golden brown on the bottom.
4. Add a few tablespoons of water to the pan and cover to steam the gyoza for 5 minutes.
5. Serve hot with soy sauce for dipping.

Tonkotsu Ramen

Ingredients:

- 4 cups pork bone broth
- 2 servings ramen noodles
- 2 slices chashu pork
- 1 soft-boiled egg
- 1/4 cup bamboo shoots, sliced
- 2 green onions, chopped
- 1 tsp sesame oil
- 1 tbsp soy sauce
- 1 tbsp mirin

Instructions:

1. Cook ramen noodles according to package instructions. Drain and set aside.
2. Heat the pork bone broth in a pot and season with soy sauce and mirin.
3. In a bowl, place the cooked noodles and pour the hot broth over them.
4. Top with chashu pork, soft-boiled egg, bamboo shoots, and green onions.
5. Drizzle with sesame oil and serve hot.

Seared Scallops with Soy Sauce

Ingredients:

- 8 scallops
- 1 tbsp vegetable oil
- 1 tbsp soy sauce
- 1 tsp rice vinegar
- 1 tsp honey
- 1/4 tsp sesame oil
- 1/4 tsp ginger, grated
- 1 tbsp green onions, chopped

Instructions:

1. Heat vegetable oil in a pan over medium-high heat.
2. Season scallops with salt and pepper, then sear them for 2-3 minutes per side until golden brown.
3. In a small bowl, mix soy sauce, rice vinegar, honey, sesame oil, and grated ginger.
4. Drizzle the sauce over the seared scallops and garnish with chopped green onions.
5. Serve immediately.

Crab Croquette

Ingredients:

- 1/2 lb crab meat
- 2 tbsp mayonnaise
- 1 tbsp Dijon mustard
- 1/2 cup panko breadcrumbs
- 1 egg, beaten
- 1/4 cup flour
- Vegetable oil for frying
- Salt and pepper, to taste

Instructions:

1. In a bowl, mix crab meat, mayonnaise, Dijon mustard, salt, and pepper.
2. Form the mixture into small patties, then coat them in flour, dip in the beaten egg, and coat with panko breadcrumbs.
3. Heat oil in a pan over medium-high heat and fry the croquettes until golden brown (2-3 minutes per side).
4. Drain on paper towels and serve hot.

Tori Katsu (Chicken Cutlet)

Ingredients:

- 2 boneless, skinless chicken breasts
- 1/2 cup all-purpose flour
- 1 egg, beaten
- 1 cup panko breadcrumbs
- Vegetable oil for frying
- Tonkatsu sauce (for serving)

Instructions:

1. Flatten the chicken breasts to an even thickness using a meat mallet.
2. Dredge the chicken in flour, dip in beaten egg, and coat with panko breadcrumbs.
3. Heat oil in a pan over medium-high heat and fry the chicken until golden brown and cooked through (5-6 minutes per side).
4. Drain on paper towels and serve with tonkatsu sauce.

Ikura Don (Salmon Roe Rice Bowl)

Ingredients:

- 1 cup sushi rice, cooked and seasoned
- 1/2 cup ikura (salmon roe)
- 1 tbsp soy sauce
- 1 tsp mirin
- 1 sheet nori (seaweed), cut into strips
- 1/4 tsp sesame seeds

Instructions:

1. In a bowl, place a serving of sushi rice.
2. Top with ikura (salmon roe).
3. Drizzle with soy sauce and mirin, and sprinkle with sesame seeds.
4. Garnish with nori strips and serve immediately.

Uni Sushi (Sea Urchin)

Ingredients:

- Sushi rice, seasoned
- 4-6 pieces of fresh uni (sea urchin)
- 1 sheet nori (seaweed)
- Soy sauce (for dipping)

Instructions:

1. Mold small amounts of sushi rice into oval-shaped portions.
2. Place a piece of uni on top of each rice portion.
3. Wrap each piece with a small strip of nori.
4. Serve with soy sauce for dipping.

Tamago (Japanese Omelette)

Ingredients:

- 4 large eggs
- 2 tbsp sugar
- 1 tbsp soy sauce
- 1 tbsp mirin
- 1/2 tsp salt
- 1 tbsp vegetable oil
- Bamboo mat for rolling (optional)

Instructions:

1. In a bowl, whisk together the eggs, sugar, soy sauce, mirin, and salt.
2. Heat a rectangular pan over low heat and brush with oil.
3. Pour a thin layer of egg mixture into the pan and cook until set. Roll the omelette up from one side and push it to the edge of the pan.
4. Add another thin layer of egg mixture, lifting the rolled omelette so the uncooked egg flows underneath. Repeat the process until all the egg mixture is used.
5. Allow the omelette to cool slightly before slicing into thick pieces. Serve as a topping for sushi or as a dish on its own.

Ebi Nigiri (Shrimp Sushi)

Ingredients:

- 2-3 large shrimp (cooked, peeled, and deveined)
- 2 cups sushi rice, cooked and seasoned
- 2 tbsp rice vinegar
- 1 tsp sugar
- 1/4 tsp salt
- Soy sauce (for dipping)

Instructions:

1. Cook the sushi rice according to package instructions and mix with rice vinegar, sugar, and salt.
2. Shape small portions of sushi rice into oval-shaped balls.
3. Gently press a shrimp onto the top of each rice ball.
4. Optionally, lightly brush the shrimp with a little soy sauce or wasabi.
5. Serve with additional soy sauce for dipping.

Miso-Marinated Eggplant

Ingredients:

- 2 medium eggplants
- 3 tbsp white miso paste
- 1 tbsp mirin
- 1 tbsp soy sauce
- 1 tbsp sesame oil
- 1 tsp sugar
- 1/4 tsp sesame seeds (for garnish)

Instructions:

1. Slice the eggplant into 1-inch thick rounds.
2. In a bowl, mix miso paste, mirin, soy sauce, sesame oil, and sugar to make the marinade.
3. Place the eggplant slices in the marinade and let them sit for 30 minutes.
4. Heat a pan over medium heat and cook the eggplant until tender and golden on both sides (about 3-4 minutes per side).
5. Garnish with sesame seeds and serve.

Ikura Chawanmushi

Ingredients:

- 2 large eggs
- 1 1/2 cups dashi broth
- 1 tbsp soy sauce
- 1 tbsp mirin
- 1/4 tsp salt
- 2 tbsp ikura (salmon roe)
- 2 tbsp shiitake mushrooms, thinly sliced
- 1 tbsp green onions, chopped

Instructions:

1. In a bowl, whisk together eggs, dashi broth, soy sauce, mirin, and salt.
2. Strain the mixture through a fine mesh sieve to remove any bubbles or impurities.
3. Pour the egg mixture into small heatproof cups, then add a few slices of shiitake mushrooms into each cup.
4. Steam the cups over medium heat for 15-20 minutes, or until set.
5. Garnish each cup with ikura and green onions before serving.

Lobster Tempura

Ingredients:

- 2 lobster tails
- 1 cup tempura flour
- 1 egg
- 1/2 cup ice-cold water
- Vegetable oil for frying
- Salt for seasoning
- Soy sauce (for dipping)

Instructions:

1. Cut the lobster tails in half lengthwise and remove the meat.
2. In a bowl, whisk together the tempura flour, egg, and ice-cold water to make the batter.
3. Heat the oil in a deep pan to 350°F (175°C).
4. Dip the lobster meat in the batter and fry until golden and crispy (about 2-3 minutes).
5. Drain on paper towels, season with salt, and serve with soy sauce for dipping.

Yuba (Tofu Skin) with Ponzu Sauce

Ingredients:

- 1 package of fresh yuba (tofu skin)
- 2 tbsp ponzu sauce
- 1 tsp sesame oil
- 1 tsp toasted sesame seeds
- 1/2 tsp chili flakes (optional)

Instructions:

1. Gently warm the yuba in a pot of hot water for 2-3 minutes, then drain.
2. Arrange the yuba on a plate and drizzle with ponzu sauce and sesame oil.
3. Sprinkle with sesame seeds and chili flakes (optional) for extra flavor.
4. Serve as an appetizer or side dish.

Oysters with Ponzu Sauce

Ingredients:

- 6 fresh oysters (shucked)
- 2 tbsp ponzu sauce
- 1 tsp grated daikon radish
- 1 tsp sliced green onions
- 1 tsp chili flakes (optional)

Instructions:

1. Arrange the oysters on a plate, ensuring they are on their half shells.
2. Drizzle ponzu sauce over the oysters.
3. Top with a small amount of grated daikon radish and green onions.
4. Optionally, add chili flakes for a spicy kick.
5. Serve immediately as a refreshing appetizer.

Agedashi Tofu

Ingredients:

- 1 block firm tofu
- 1/4 cup cornstarch
- 1/4 cup soy sauce
- 1 tbsp mirin
- 1 tbsp dashi
- 1/2 tsp grated ginger
- 2 tbsp green onions, chopped
- 1 tbsp bonito flakes (optional)
- Vegetable oil for frying

Instructions:

1. Cut the tofu into bite-sized cubes and pat dry with paper towels.
2. Dredge the tofu cubes in cornstarch, shaking off any excess.
3. Heat oil in a pan over medium heat and fry the tofu until golden brown (about 2-3 minutes).
4. In a separate bowl, mix soy sauce, mirin, dashi, and grated ginger to make the sauce.
5. Place the fried tofu in a bowl, pour the sauce over it, and garnish with green onions and bonito flakes.

Hokkaido King Crab Legs

Ingredients:

- 2 Hokkaido king crab legs
- 2 tbsp butter
- 1 tbsp lemon juice
- 1 tbsp garlic, minced
- 1 tbsp chopped parsley
- Salt and pepper to taste

Instructions:

1. Steam or boil the king crab legs until heated through (about 5-7 minutes).
2. In a small pan, melt butter and sauté garlic until fragrant.
3. Add lemon juice, parsley, salt, and pepper to the butter mixture.
4. Serve the crab legs with the garlic butter sauce for dipping.

Sea Bass in Yuzu Soy Sauce

Ingredients:

- 2 sea bass fillets
- 2 tbsp soy sauce
- 1 tbsp yuzu juice
- 1 tbsp mirin
- 1 tsp sesame oil
- 1 tsp sliced green onions
- 1 tsp toasted sesame seeds

Instructions:

1. In a small bowl, mix soy sauce, yuzu juice, mirin, and sesame oil to make the sauce.
2. Heat a pan over medium heat and sear the sea bass fillets on both sides until golden and cooked through (about 3-4 minutes per side).
3. Drizzle the yuzu soy sauce over the fish and garnish with sliced green onions and sesame seeds.
4. Serve immediately with rice or vegetables.

Japanese Beef Katsu

Ingredients:

- 2 beef tenderloin steaks (or sirloin)
- 1/2 cup all-purpose flour
- 2 large eggs, beaten
- 1 cup panko breadcrumbs
- 1/4 cup vegetable oil
- Salt and pepper to taste
- Tonkatsu sauce for serving

Instructions:

1. Season the beef steaks with salt and pepper on both sides.
2. Dredge each steak in flour, dip in the beaten eggs, and then coat in panko breadcrumbs.
3. Heat the vegetable oil in a pan over medium-high heat. Fry the beef steaks for about 3-4 minutes per side, or until golden and crispy.
4. Drain on paper towels and slice into strips.
5. Serve with tonkatsu sauce on the side.

Sushi Rolls with Truffle Oil

Ingredients:

- 2 cups sushi rice, cooked and seasoned
- 10 sheets nori (seaweed)
- 1/2 lb fresh tuna or salmon, thinly sliced
- 1/2 cucumber, julienned
- 1/2 avocado, sliced
- 1 tbsp truffle oil
- Soy sauce for dipping

Instructions:

1. Lay a sheet of nori on a bamboo sushi mat, shiny side down.
2. Spread a thin layer of sushi rice evenly on the nori, leaving about 1 inch at the top free of rice.
3. Place slices of tuna or salmon, cucumber, and avocado in a line across the center of the rice.
4. Drizzle a small amount of truffle oil over the ingredients.
5. Roll the sushi tightly using the sushi mat, then slice into bite-sized pieces.
6. Serve with soy sauce for dipping.

Kurage (Jellyfish) Salad

Ingredients:

- 1 cup pre-cooked jellyfish (available at Asian markets)
- 1/2 cucumber, julienned
- 1/2 red bell pepper, julienned
- 2 tbsp rice vinegar
- 1 tbsp sesame oil
- 1 tsp soy sauce
- 1 tsp sugar
- 1 tbsp sesame seeds
- 1 tsp chopped cilantro (optional)

Instructions:

1. Rinse the jellyfish and drain thoroughly.
2. In a small bowl, mix rice vinegar, sesame oil, soy sauce, and sugar to make the dressing.
3. Toss the jellyfish, cucumber, and bell pepper with the dressing.
4. Garnish with sesame seeds and cilantro.
5. Serve chilled as a refreshing appetizer.

Dashi Soup with Tofu

Ingredients:

- 4 cups dashi stock (homemade or from dashi powder)
- 1/2 block tofu, cubed
- 1/4 cup soy sauce
- 1 tbsp mirin
- 1 tsp sesame oil
- 2 green onions, chopped
- 1 tsp grated ginger

Instructions:

1. Heat the dashi stock in a pot over medium heat.
2. Add the soy sauce, mirin, and sesame oil to the pot.
3. Gently add the cubed tofu and simmer for 3-4 minutes.
4. Garnish with chopped green onions and grated ginger before serving.

Shoyu Ramen with Soft-Boiled Egg

Ingredients:

- 4 cups chicken broth
- 2 cups water
- 3 tbsp soy sauce
- 1 tbsp miso paste
- 1 tbsp mirin
- 2 servings ramen noodles
- 2 soft-boiled eggs (boiled for 6-7 minutes)
- 2-3 slices chashu pork (optional)
- 2 green onions, chopped
- 1 tbsp sesame seeds
- 1 sheet nori (for garnish)

Instructions:

1. In a large pot, bring the chicken broth and water to a boil. Add soy sauce, miso paste, and mirin, then reduce to a simmer.
2. Cook the ramen noodles according to package instructions, then drain.
3. Divide the cooked noodles into bowls and pour the hot broth over them.
4. Top each bowl with a soft-boiled egg, chashu pork, green onions, sesame seeds, and nori.
5. Serve immediately.

Kani Salad (Crab Salad)

Ingredients:

- 1 cup imitation crab meat, shredded
- 1/2 cucumber, julienned
- 1/4 cup mayonnaise
- 1 tbsp rice vinegar
- 1 tsp sesame oil
- 1/2 tsp sugar
- 1 tsp sriracha (optional)
- 1 tbsp sesame seeds
- 1 tbsp chopped cilantro

Instructions:

1. In a bowl, mix the shredded crab meat and cucumber.
2. In a separate bowl, whisk together mayonnaise, rice vinegar, sesame oil, sugar, and sriracha (if using).
3. Toss the crab mixture with the dressing until well combined.
4. Garnish with sesame seeds and chopped cilantro.
5. Serve chilled.

Shrimp and Vegetable Tempura Udon

Ingredients:

- 2 servings udon noodles
- 6-8 large shrimp, peeled and deveined
- 1/2 cup zucchini, sliced into thin rounds
- 1/2 cup sweet potato, sliced into thin rounds
- 1/2 cup tempura flour
- 1 egg
- 1/2 cup cold water
- Vegetable oil for frying
- 2 cups dashi broth
- 2 tbsp soy sauce
- 1 tbsp mirin
- 1 tsp sesame oil

Instructions:

1. Cook the udon noodles according to package instructions and set aside.
2. In a bowl, mix tempura flour, egg, and cold water to create the batter.
3. Heat vegetable oil in a deep pan to 350°F (175°C).
4. Dip the shrimp, zucchini, and sweet potato into the batter and fry until golden and crispy, about 2-3 minutes.
5. In a separate pot, heat dashi broth with soy sauce, mirin, and sesame oil.
6. Serve the udon noodles in bowls, pour the hot broth over them, and top with tempura shrimp and vegetables.

Tataki-style Tuna

Ingredients:

- 1 lb sushi-grade tuna, seared on the outside and rare on the inside
- 1 tbsp sesame oil
- 2 tbsp soy sauce
- 1 tbsp rice vinegar
- 1 tbsp grated ginger
- 1 tbsp sesame seeds
- 1 tbsp chopped green onions

Instructions:

1. Heat a pan over medium-high heat and sear the tuna for 1-2 minutes on each side, leaving the center rare.
2. Slice the tuna thinly against the grain.
3. Mix sesame oil, soy sauce, rice vinegar, and grated ginger in a small bowl.
4. Drizzle the sauce over the sliced tuna and sprinkle with sesame seeds and chopped green onions.
5. Serve immediately as an appetizer or entrée.

Chilled Soba with Tsuyu Sauce

Ingredients:

- 2 servings soba noodles
- 1/4 cup soy sauce
- 2 tbsp mirin
- 1/4 cup dashi stock
- 1 tbsp sesame seeds
- 2 green onions, chopped
- 1 tsp wasabi (optional)

Instructions:

1. Cook the soba noodles according to package instructions and rinse under cold water to chill.
2. In a bowl, mix soy sauce, mirin, and dashi stock to make the tsuyu sauce.
3. Serve the chilled soba noodles with the sauce on the side, garnished with sesame seeds, green onions, and optional wasabi.

Gyu Kushi (Grilled Beef Skewers)

Ingredients:

- 1 lb beef sirloin, cut into bite-sized cubes
- 2 tbsp soy sauce
- 1 tbsp mirin
- 1 tbsp sake
- 1 tbsp sesame oil
- 1 tbsp honey
- 1/2 tsp garlic powder
- 1/4 tsp black pepper
- Skewers (wooden or metal)

Instructions:

1. Soak the skewers in water for 30 minutes (if using wooden skewers).
2. In a bowl, whisk together soy sauce, mirin, sake, sesame oil, honey, garlic powder, and black pepper to make the marinade.
3. Thread the beef cubes onto the skewers and place them in the marinade for 30 minutes.
4. Preheat a grill or grill pan over medium-high heat.
5. Grill the skewers for 3-4 minutes per side or until cooked to your desired level of doneness.
6. Serve with a side of rice or vegetables.

www.ingramcontent.com/pod-product-compliance
Lightning Source LLC
LaVergne TN
LVHW081340060526
838201LV00055B/2763